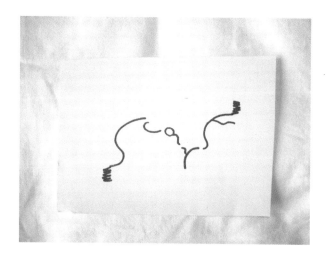

Editor's Note

Reading accounts from the sailors of the past, you get the overwhelming feeling that most took refuge in the sense of placelessness that the sea afforded. You were, of course, suspended in time as well; an occassional letter from home at Manila or Ceylon might be your only engagement with the narrative minutae of the land. You were, to all intents and purposes, floating. Maybe the times of selective ignorance are behind us, subsumed by an all encompassing awareness of our own presence at all times. You may ask, in our McWorld of Americanisms, why bother moving at all? We move because we long for the fragmentary glances where we recognise ourselves. We move because we are sure the figs taste better over there. Or maybe we just move because we have to and because we hope. The second edition of SCARF deals with the stories and accounts of people who were compelled to question their relationship with their surroundings. Whether Antonio's 'Nowhere' or Onyeabor's 'Everywhere', each piece points to places where unwritten futures coalesce and dance illuminate.

The Atomic Bomb!

Nick Richards

As a music fan, it is very easy to let certain tropes prevail to create a sense of order or continuity. There's the tortured genius (Elliott Smith, Kurt Cobain etc), the arrogant rocker (The Gallaghers) or the middle class wannabe (I wanna sleep with Common People!). However, trying to compartmentalise a 70's proto-techno, synth, funk and afro-psychedelic producer from provincial Nigeria, rumoured to be funded by the Soviet Union is unlikely to be a fruitful endeavour. Maybe the 'surreal villain in a second rate Roger Moore film' archetype applies here (The Synth Who Loved Me?). Probably not. William Onyeabor was, and is, singular.

I can imagine the trepidation in the mind of Eric Welles-Nyström, a curator at New York based Luaka Bop Records, when he finally dialled the number of the Onyeabor residency. Which character was going to answer when it rang?

"I only want to speak about God. I don't want to go back to that time."

Welles-Nyström put the phone down. Trying to unravel the Onyeaborian webb was going to require a lot more than an international call. It seemed he had to get through God first.

Before Luaka Bop made contact with him, all that was known was that there was a complex and reclusive man who single handedly brought the future to Africa. The crate digging community, spurred on by a proliferation of interest in African records in the early 2000's, still knew nothing beyond hearsay. Music professionals had very little contact with him as he meticulously controlled every aspect of recording, production and distribution.

Even the everyday people of Enugu knew nothing, driving past his flamboyant palace on the outskirts of town with the gate always shut. People from vastly different backgrounds wanted to know: Who is William Onyeabor?

His early life was marked by poverty and social upheaval. In 1960, when Onyeabor was 14, Nigeria celebrated independence from the British government - ostensibly ending the long imperial influence in Africa for good. The transition to self-governance came with many teething problems, which likely formed Onyeabor's scathing political messages against instability and imbalance of power.

After this point, his timeline has more holes than a string vest.

He first travelled to Scandinavia before moving to Soviet Moscow to study film making and record manufacturing - although it is also rumoured he studied Law at Oxford under a pseudonym at this time. By 1978, he had returned from the USSR with the financial means to assemble his own studio and label, as well as a pressing plant with a complete workforce. After 1985, he retreated from the music world and, so it seemed, life itself. Where did he get the money from? Where did he get the equipment from? What sort of link did he actually have with the Russians?

In 1987, he was named West African Industrialist of the Year, an indication of his shrewd business acumen. It's possible on this strength alone he was able to fund his creative pursuits, but it doesn't answer the question of where in rural West Africa he found synthesisers more advanced than most elite Western studios at the time. Maybe Brezhnev personally shipped the Moog that created the acidic opening to songs like 'Let's Fall in Love'.

These questions, amongst many others, inspired Welles-Nystrom and a Vice documentary crew to travel to Enugu and visit the man simply known as the 'Chief'. Through the help of Goddy Oku and numerous other connections in Africa, a meeting was set at the Palais de Onyeabor. Uchenna Ikonne, a Nigerian-American music journalist and crucial point of contact throughout, offered these words of warning to Welles-Nyström before the meeting: 'If you go there, he's going to break your neck. He's going to ask where the money is.'

Brezhnev Comes Courting

Leonid
Brezhnev

When Welles-Nyström nervously sat down in the living room, he was introduced to a man called T.B. Joshua. The man wasn't in the room. He was a Nigerian prophet blasting from the TV that Onyeabor sat in front of, transfixed. He would be mediating the exchanges from now on. Welles-Nyström must've been taken aback by this resolute faith, but very quickly Onyeabor's internationalism emerged. From CNN to Al-Jazeera to an English-speaking Chinese news broadcast before returning to T.B. Joshua, every conversation he had with Onyeabor was accompanied by the sounds of the world.

When it came to answering the questions that brought Luaka Bop and Vice to Enugu in the first place, the Chief's openness was variable. He indulged in tales of travels around the globe, including the story behind the picture on the cover of his album 'Hypertension' taken at Tivoli Gardens in Copenhagen. He'd even been to Sweden (Welles-Nyström's homeland). He showed wit and humour, even going as far as calling himself Eric's African Dad. Crucially though, he was belligerent when the subject of Russia came up, or what inspired him to make, and then quit, music. These loose ends, it seemed, would not be tied.

Most true originators, which Onyeabor undoubtedly is, revel in their past creations, whether overtly or concealed through image. Maybe religion muddies the waters in these situations, but one gets the feeling that despite professions of Christian servitude, Onyeabor was immensely proud of his former international music and outlook. In fact, it was more obvious than he ever realised.

He holds the records, and I can tell this is the first time in a really long time that he's actually holding these things. And he's flipping the records and he's going through the songs, one by one, reminiscing really magically. "These were the songs I did." And he very, very proudly points to the corner of the record with his logo, "Printed by Wilfilms Ltd." And he says, "This was my company. I did everything. I made this"

At first, the proverbial door was shut on Luaka Bop Records, only to be marginally reopened by relentless investigation and curiosity. It remains to be seen whether anyone in the future will be capable of kicking down the door entirely.

WILLIAM ONYEABOR 1946 - 2017

Sacrificial Wallows
Bosco Sodi

I've heard of wasps gouge themselves to wallow in the
scent of a fig
Read of fair men and disheartened genius débase
themselves for white armed and richly tressed women
Seen gentle pearl white insurgents gasp in relief
to have bathed in their blood.
caressing upright their favorite quill

I know that If you touched the surface of the water,
you'd jump in to drown inside the ripples
That you'd claw at your wrists
Or swallow your own hand
To wallow in your beauty

it's the sole movement that doesn't ask why
And for that you'd give it your soul
For to wallow as you have
one need not sagacity
For beauty is taciturn
But bares it's breasts and by the very motion begs you
to leave marks

Estrangement that feeds lines
lines that feed connection
I whisper to you softly
I'd like to write something life changing
And you say
I just want to write something beautiful

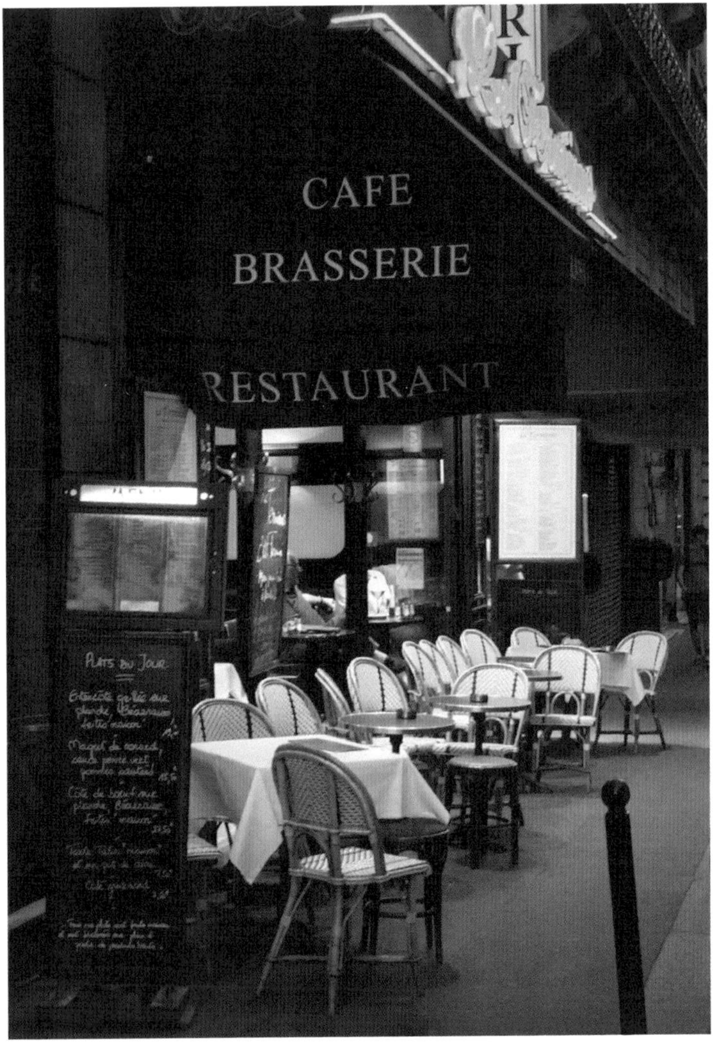
CAFE
BRASSERIE
RESTAURANT

Chez Marie

In the lower east side of the city, a car pulls into the carpark of a long-established French restaurant. The restaurant is well loved by the city's residents for its good food and warm atmosphere. Inside the car is a man and a woman. They are having an argument.

'What do you mean you're done?'
The car was silent; Serena just stared out of the window. They'd arrived at the parking lot and Matthew came to a jerky stop. He always braked too late for his driving to be considered smooth. Street lights illuminated Serena's back in a soft white glow as it faced him. He was ready to get angry again, but he stopped himself.
'Do you recognise this? I booked here specifically.'
She didn't reply. She didn't even turn around, so he carried on. His voice was quieter now, softer.
'This is where we tried to go for that meal, last winter. Chez Marie. We didn't know that it was closed and we walked all the way here. Just as we got here it started raining and neither of us had a coat and we got fucking soaked.'
Matthew tried to gently turn Serena around to face him. She shrugged him off, and his arm fell back down to his lap.

'Do you remember? We sheltered in that doorway. I kept apologising but you said you didn't care. You said you were just happy to be out with me.'

Matthew broke off for a second. Serena could barely hear him now. It was like he was struggling to get the words out.

'That's when you first told me you loved me.'

Serena watched the tired restaurant front. Why was Matthew bringing her back here, now? The city was littered with places that he could ascribe some sort of meaning to, if he really wanted.

Like the park they went to on their fifth date, sometime last November when the frost hung thick over the lake, and they skirted slowly around it, talking and holding hands. Or under the covers of his bed, where they would hide, her head rising and falling as she lay on his chest. Or the bar where they first met - he'd tried to take her back that night but she'd given him her number and a smile goodnight instead. Or the park this summer where he'd undermined her in front of her friends and she had felt stupid and embarrassed. Or the tower on the top of the hill, overlooking the frosty city, where he'd nervously asked her to be his girlfriend. Or the museum they went to late this spring, where they'd walked around separately and barely talked at all; they'd had some sort of argument on the way. Or here, now.

She turned back to look at him. He looked back at her with that concerned face he sometimes wore, that made it look like he was squinting. His handsome, crooked nose and the light stubble that made him seem older than he was. Those big, dull, hazel eyes. The ones that used to shine so bright.

They were back to where they had started but so much had changed.
'Just take me home please, Matt', she said.

Inside the restaurant, an elderly lady's hands shake as she reads the menu. All the chairs at the table are in use, apart from one, on the left-hand side of the elderly lady.

The chair has been left empty on purpose.

Mamie's hands shook as she took La Carte and examined it. Every time they went, she'd do the routine. First, she'd slowly put on her glasses - that hung on a chain around her neck - and scrutinise the menu. Her lips would move silently as she read, tilting her head backwards to peer down through the glasses that clung onto her nose. Then, she would exclaim 'Cassoulet! I used to have that as a child,' - as if she was surprised that it was on the menu at all. Maybe she was, nowadays; her memory wasn't as good as it had once been.

'I think I will be having this..'. She would say, turning to Celeste and Paul. 'Very traditional. In l'Occitan, I grew up on this. This dish is in your blood.'. Mamie always ordered Cassoulet, and she always told her grandchildren that it was a part of their heritage. It had become ritual at this point.

At some point, when Paul and Celine were very young, Mamie had triumphantly announced that Chez Marie was the most authentic French restaurant in town, and her word was final. Every family event since had taken place at their dimly lit table at Chez Marie. Paul's confirmation had tasted like chargrilled steak frites, served pink on the inside and coated in a rich, garlicky butter - Celine's had tasted like brothy, fishy Bouillabaisse and so much fresh baguette she had almost been sick. Once she'd decided that they were old enough, Mamie started to discreetly pour them out small glasses of warming, metallic red wine.

Papie always used to sit on the left hand side of Mamie, with a big glass of brandy. He was a lot quieter than Mamie - she did the talking for the two of them. His big, leathery hand would rest on the back of Mamie's chair as he sipped his drink. He loved her very much. Papie didn't say lots, but the way he used to look at Mamie said it all.

This meal was the first time that Mamie was wheeled into the restaurant. Her legs got tired if she was on them for too long, and she had taken a few bad falls recently. On the car ride there, she fiercely cursed the wheelchair. 'I do not need it, but your mother insists.' she explained to Paul and Celine, wrinkled lips grinning. Mamie was getting noticeably older, but during the meal she still managed to put away more wine than Paul and Celine could handle. She was as argumentative as ever, and even though she'd started to repeat herself, the table hung on to her every word. She had a knack for storytelling and a love for embellishments. Whenever the rest of the family disputed something she'd said, they somehow ended up all being wrong. Mamie was always right. They talked for hours about holidays long gone, childhood stories, Papie, France, and Mamie's newest favourite topic – the bloody wheelchair.

When the meal ended, Mamie called over Paul and Celine. She reached into her green leather purse - the one she'd owned since they were children - and handed them a five pound note each. Paul had a stable job in marketing, just outside of the city, and Celine's bakery, Le Pain de Mamie, was just starting to make a profit. They embarrassedly accepted Mamie's gift and wheeled her back to the car. 'I am tired,' Mamie announced. 'Me too' Celine said reassuringly.

They helped her into the front seat of their mother's car and closed the door. Celine gave Paul a hug. 'I'll see you at the next one,' she said to him. She bent down to the window and knocked on it. 'Bye-bye Mamie. We'll take you out again soon.'

Mamie didn't answer; she had fallen asleep in the passenger seat.

It is later now. Inside the restaurant, the lights are turned off. Two people are sitting at a table, drinking together after a long shift.

'I am sorry that I shouted at you about the sauce,' Jean said to Zeina. He paused, but she knew better than to say anything. 'I expect a lot of you, I know. You are a decent cook, but you could be great.' They sipped their beers in the dark restaurant. After the last table had got up and paid, the building seemed to breathe a sigh of relief. Jean and Zeina would be back, early in the morning, to prepare for the lunch service. For now, though, all was still. The chairs lay upside down on the tables, casting long shadows against the moonlight that poured in through the window. A bucket and mop leant tiredly against the far wall, and various electronics blinked occasionally in the dark. The KP was still in the kitchen; he would be finished soon.

The rest of the kitchen staff had left hastily after the close, throwing their whites into the laundry room as they went. Only Jean and Zeina had stayed. The hot anger of the busy kitchen had disappeared, and the chef and his sous-chef sat together in tired silence.

'I shouldn't have burnt the sauce.' Zeina admitted.

Jean sighed and ran his hand through his greying hair. 'I know that you are better than that, Zeina. That's why I say these things. You were behind on prep as well today. You remind me a lot of myself at your age. I used to want it so bad.' He paused to take another sip of his pint. 'Although, I suppose it hasn't done much for me.'

'Don't start with that.' Zeina said sharply. She knew where this conversation was headed, and she didn't like it. Jean was a great mentor in many ways - a little harsh at times, granted - but she didn't like these funny moods he got into. She was comfortable at Chez Marie, and she was good at what she did.

'I know you are comfortable here,' Jean said gently. It was as if he could read her mind. 'But that is not necessarily a good thing. I am fifty-eight in a few months, and look what I have to show for it... My legs hurt all day, I have a bad back and a foul temper. I sweat all day and night in a second-class kitchen, I have no social life and nothing better to do on my days off than to hang around here getting drunk at the bar.'

'The last review was not too bad. And we've got another one coming up in a month. We're a good team. We can get out of this. And I've got loads of ideas for a new menu. We just need a bit of time to figure out a couple recipes and then we can hit the ground running, ready for the new year...' she tailed off.

'A-ha,' Jean said softly, 'even you do not believe what you are saying.' he shook his head then scanned around the dark room. He lowered his voice. 'I love this restaurant just as much as you do, Zeina. More, probably. I have poured myself into it for so long. But I have seen the records - I could show them to you if you wish. We are losing money by the day. Why do you think they are laying off so much staff at such a busy time? Why do you think we are working so many extra hours?'

Zeina knew it was bad, but could it be as bad as he said? After a drink Jean often got like this. Maybe he was right though, this time. He carried on, low and steady. 'It's your life, Zeina. I know this job means a lot to you. But you could do better. That's all I'm trying to say.'

It is much later now, and all the staff have left the restaurant. The only light that remains on is the light in the back office, past the kitchen.

The office is deadly quiet. A man is sitting at the office desk, looking through financial records. A woman walks into the room. She walks up to the man and starts gently rubbing his back.

'How is it?' Amelie asked her husband. He looked awful these days; he had big black bags under his eyes and his legs jittered uncontrollably.

'It's bad,' he said. 'I don't know what to do.' He looked up at her, almost pleading. She had no solutions to offer. All she could do was gently rub his back.

The room fell silent again. They stayed like that, husband and wife, in the back office of the restaurant they would soon lose, for a while longer.

Written by Eric Battye

Sudden Looks

Antonio Santillana

You ask me where I am from?
I reply "from nowhere"
You stare back at me startled?
I answer with nothing but kindness.
Like many others I was born in some house, on some corner of some town.
But like everybody else, I am not only from that house, not only from that corner of that town.
I also come from where the first droplets of water flow down towards the river's source. I also come from where the clouds discretely start to sail. I come from where the shrivelled autumn leaves float eternally from the tree to the ground.
Although it is important to know that I am from that place, it is also essential to know that I also come from over there.
Over there, where the huayco* thunders down from. Over there, where the ground unexpectedly shakes and tears open abruptly. Over there, where blazing bodies of magma roar violently before birthing an earthquake.
I am from both these places and so are you.

*Natural disaster specific to Perú, flash flood immediately followed by a devastating mudslide which destroys everything in its path.

Judging by your disbelieving eyes and the evident confusion in which your jaw incredulously hangs, this has all become too esoteric. Allow me to help.

You think that you don't know that place, you suppose that it is isolated in the corner of some unknown map. You think that it concealed itself between the branches as you walked by. You trust that it is like a mountain in which a thick cloud has confidently asserted itself; behind the mist.

But, in reality it is very different. It is in front of you at the same time as it is behind. It is outside as long as it can be found inside. Right now it is in my words and also in your ears. It is just a matter of listening once again. Just a matter of remembering that the cloud was not always there — it is not in its nature. Never forget that there was a time when it was all so clear, so effortless, so natural.

Because yes, it does hide. Yes, you do not see it. But like the air that surrounds you, it is undeniably invisible and yet so real.

It is found, without any strain at all, in passing looks. The attraction, fear, comfort and desire found within someone you have never seen. There, where a line starts to appear and a bridge is built, in which two souls meet and hold each other like a handshake. They recognise each other and you recognise yourself. You manage to find a part of yourself in the other. If this is not the case then how is it that someone so foreign becomes so familiar?

It is even more obvious in the conversations between complete strangers on a trip. There are no obstacles between you both; no true prejudices over the person other than those that weren't invited. Only those prejudices which are like distant parasites, remaining alien to oneself. In those remote and isolated conversations in places where the relentless pressure of duty has melted away can you find that place with even more potency. You manage to find those people who are also like you — in a pleasant state of forgetfulness — and precisely there can the long hidden memory reemerge. Precisely there can that connection exist. Forgetting is necessary for remembering.

Forget that path which you have gone down, that path where you have been pushed and kicked forward. Forget where they exiled you to and remember where you came from. Only there can you find the others who are in daily transit.

Eric Battye Edson Dibble Mark Leighton Lola Payne Nick Richards Antonio Santillana Bosco Sodi.

Printed in Great Britain
by Amazon

33773037R00023